EBOLA
OUTBREAK

BY CAROLEE LAINE

CONTENT CONSULTANT
Ana S. Ayala
Global Health Law LL.M. Program Director
Georgetown University Law Center

Essential Library

An Imprint of Abdo Publishing | abdopublishing.com

abdopublishing.com

Published by Abdo Publishing, a division of ABDO, PO Box 398166, Minneapolis, Minnesota 55439. Copyright © 2016 by Abdo Consulting Group, Inc. International copyrights reserved in all countries. No part of this book may be reproduced in any form without written permission from the publisher. Essential Library™ is a trademark and logo of Abdo Publishing.

Printed in the United States of America, North Mankato, Minnesota
082015
012016

THIS BOOK CONTAINS RECYCLED MATERIALS

Cover Photo: Jerome Delay/AP Images
Interior Photos: Dominique Faget/AFP/Getty Images, 5; Kristin Palitza/ Picture-Alliance/DPA/AP Images, 7; Youssouf Bah/AP Images, 9, 31; Abbas Dulleh/ AP Images, 12, 55; Sunday Alamba/AP Images, 15, 43; Centers for Disease Control and Prevention, 17, 20, 25, 61; Jerome Delay/AP Images, 29; Anthony Behar/ Picture-Alliance/DPA/AP Images, 34; US Army, 37; Zoom Dosso/AFP/Getty Images, 40, 91; John Spink/Atlanta Journal-Constitution/AP Images, 46; Joe Raedle/Getty Images, 49; Mladen Antonov/AFP/Getty Images, 53; Tina Susman/AP Images, 58; Cliff Owen/AP Images, 64; Richard Drew/AP Images, 67; Michael Duff/AP Images, 69; Pawel Supernak/Corbis, 73; Spencer Platt/Getty Images, 77; Robert F. Bukaty/ AP Images, 80; Kyodo/AP Images, 82, 87; Patsy Lynch/Rex/AP Images, 84; Manuel Balce Ceneta/AP Images, 88; Asahi Shimbun/Getty Images, 94; John Moore/Getty Images, 97; Issouf Sanogo/AFP/Getty Images, 99

Editor: Arnold Ringstad
Series Designer: Maggie Villaume

Library of Congress Control Number: 2015944927

Cataloging-in-Publication Data

Laine, Carolee.
 Ebola outbreak / Carolee Laine.
  p. cm. -- (Special reports)
ISBN 978-1-62403-900-3 (lib. bdg.)
Includes bibliographical references and index.
1. Epidemiology--Juvenile literature.   2. Disease outbreaks--Juvenile literature.
I. Title.
614.4--dc23

                                                  2015944927

CONTENTS

CHAPTER ONE

OUTBREAK
2014

The name *Ebola* calls to mind images of fear, suffering, and medical heroism. But before 2014, most people knew little about the now-familiar disease. Within a few months of Ebola's spread, it became one of the top international news stories of the year. The outbreak of 2014 killed thousands of people. It began with one case in West Africa.

PATIENT ZERO

The first known person to suffer from a disease in a particular outbreak is known as patient zero. For the 2014 Ebola outbreak, patient zero was a two-year-old boy living in the West African nation of Guinea. On December 6, 2013, he died after suffering for four days

Images of health-care workers in heavy protective gear became common in the media as the virus spread.

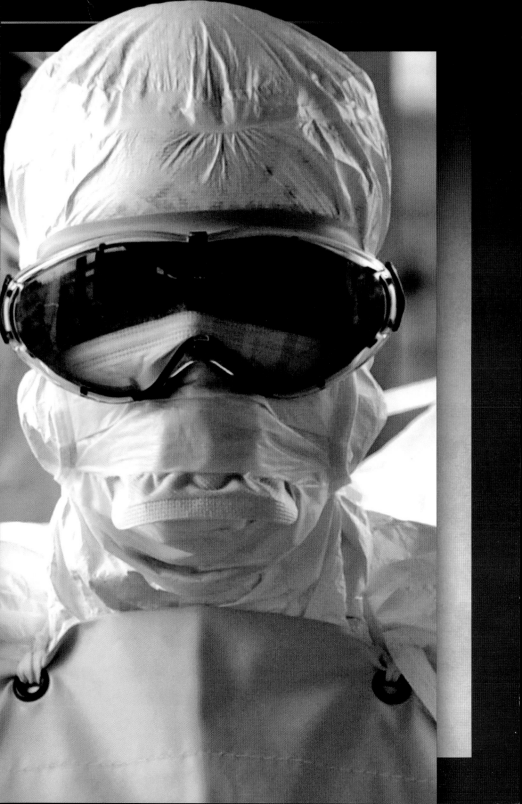

PERSONAL PROTECTION

Because Ebola can be highly contagious when people come in contact with the bodily fluids of an infected patient, health-care workers are at risk for catching the disease. To stay safe, they require extensive clothing and equipment, including a scrub suit, rubber boots, a waterproof gown, a medical mask, protective goggles or a face shield, a head covering, and rubber gloves that extend over the sleeves of the gown. To remain effective, the protective gear has to be put on and taken off in a certain order. This process is supervised by fellow health-care workers to ensure safety.

Many health-care workers in West Africa lacked even the most basic protective gear during the 2014 crisis. In August 2014, a *Wall Street Journal* article noted, "Health workers have been treating many patients with unprotected hands, greatly increasing the risk the Ebola virus will kill the very professionals trying to fight it."[1]

with an unidentified illness. A week later, his mother died. Within a short time, his three-year-old sister and his grandmother also died. Two mourners at the grandmother's funeral unknowingly carried the disease back to their village.

A health worker in the mourners' village became ill and carried the disease to his own village. The health worker and his doctor both died, and both of them infected relatives who lived nearby. By the time the illness was diagnosed as Ebola virus disease, the virus had killed dozens in Guinea. New cases were appearing in the neighboring countries of Liberia and Sierra Leone. From patient zero in Guinea, Ebola virus disease spread rapidly through three of West Africa's poorest countries.

Ebola was able to quickly infect many people in Guinea and other areas without modern medical facilities.

BREAKING THE CHAIN OF INFECTION

Ebola virus disease has no known cure, and by early 2015 no government-approved vaccine existed to prevent it. Health systems had to use other ways to control the spread of the disease. The process involved isolating people who were infected and monitoring everyone who had come in contact with an infected person. Anyone in the monitored group who became sick would then be isolated. By doing so, health-care workers hoped to break the chain of infection. Without any healthy people to infect, the disease would stop spreading.

OUTBREAKS AND EPIDEMICS

An outbreak of a contagious disease happens when more cases than expected occur in a particular place or population over a given amount of time. An epidemic happens when a disease spreads rapidly to many people. To epidemiologists, an outbreak and an epidemic are similar. But to the general public, the term *epidemic* often implies a more serious situation. An outbreak or epidemic alerts health authorities to take precautions and educate people to prevent the spread of disease. The term *pandemic* refers to a widespread disease that affects people across different parts of the world. In 1918, an influenza pandemic killed tens of millions of people and spread to every populated continent.

The task of controlling the spread of the disease in West Africa became overwhelming for the small village hospitals and limited health-care resources of the affected region. Medical centers lacked sufficient doctors, nurses, and epidemiologists. So many people became ill it was impossible to isolate them, much less trace all their contacts. Many health workers did not have the necessary training to recognize the disease. They were not equipped with the proper gear to protect themselves or prevent other patients from becoming infected.

A lack of knowledge about Ebola made the situation worse. Health workers attempted to educate the public by warning people not to touch anyone who was ill. But people continued caring for their family members, thereby spreading the disease. Some delayed seeking treatment when they were sick. They had heard negative stories about treatment centers. They knew that many people who went for treatment did not come out alive. Other people hid relatives who were sick so they would not be isolated from their families. A traditional belief that illness was a punishment for wrongdoing prevented some sick people from seeking help. Many turned to traditional faith healers. These were not medical professionals, and they often did more harm than good.

In the early phase of the outbreak, international aid workers educated people about Ebola in an attempt to quell fears based on rumors.

Fear of doctors and outsiders contributed to the spread of the disease. People began to blame them for bringing Ebola to their communities. They set up barriers to prevent health workers from entering their villages. They refused treatment, ignored warnings, and even threatened the workers who came to help them. An angry mob attacked an Ebola treatment facility in Guinea, and security forces were called to control a crowd that tried to break out of isolation in Liberia.

INADEQUATE RESOURCES

In March and April 2014, the disease seemed to be under control. This gave people a false sense of confidence. Then the outbreak began spreading again, much worse than it had before. The rate of new cases outpaced the ability of health workers to keep track of them. The number of new patients far exceeded the number of beds in hospitals and clinics. Health-care providers were overworked, and many began falling ill themselves.

Conditions in most health-care facilities were poor. For example, at a hospital in Guinea's capital, Conakry, treatment rooms were poorly lit and had no sinks.

Sanitation consisted of a few buckets of chlorine solution. It was impossible for staff to clean their hands between patients. Sometimes patients who were gravely ill with Ebola were in the same room with patients who had died from it and patients who had other diseases. In Sierra Leone, Ebola patients were kept at holding centers, where they received little care, until space became available at distant treatment centers. These patients posed a serious risk of infection to the health workers and soldiers who guarded them.

Health-care workers lacked adequate training in how to prevent the spread of Ebola. They did not know how to protect themselves from the disease. They did their best to

TOO FEW DOCTORS

Health systems in West Africa were extremely limited even before the Ebola outbreak. One way to study the level of health care in a country is to compare the number of doctors with the overall population. For example, at the time of the Ebola outbreak in Liberia, Sierra Leone, and Guinea, these areas had approximately 1 or 2 doctors per 100,000 people. By comparison, the United States has approximately 245 doctors per 100,000 people.[2]

In 2014, the addition of hundreds of patients quickly overwhelmed hospitals in the countries hardest hit by the Ebola virus. Nurses worked 12-hour days under the most difficult conditions, and they did not receive the hazard pay they were promised. Many stopped coming to work. Shortages of protective gear and lack of adequate training resulted in the deaths of many health-care workers. A Red Cross supervisor in Liberia issued a plea to organizations, regional governments, and the international community. He said, "We know how to stop Ebola, but we need help."[3]

The fear of Ebola spread through West Africa in the summer of 2014.

care for patients based on limited training presentations from their superiors. They desperately needed basic supplies: sterile syringes, aspirin, chlorine for disinfectant solutions, protective suits and gloves, and sugar and salt solutions. They also needed body bags to safely remove the bodies of Ebola victims.

OUT OF CONTROL

In July, a medical charity working in West Africa declared Ebola "out of control."[4] In August, the World Health Organization (WHO) called the Ebola epidemic a "public health emergency of international concern."[5] This designation triggered an international response to contain the outbreak. Several African countries neighboring the affected nations closed their borders. Airlines suspended flights to the area.

Ebola virus disease had been discovered 40 years before the 2014 outbreak. Several other outbreaks had occurred in recent decades, and each had been controlled within a few months. Epidemiologists sought to understand what made this outbreak so much deadlier than the others.

"WORKERS WERE FAILING TO TRACE ALL PATIENTS' CONTACTS. THE RESULTING UNSUSPECTED CASES, APPEARING AT HOSPITALS WITHOUT STANDARD INFECTION CONTROL MEASURES, WORSENED THE SPREAD IN A 'VICIOUS CIRCLE.'"[6]

—DR. SIMON MARDEL, BRITISH EMERGENCY PHYSICIAN SENT TO GUINEA

FROM THE
HEADLINES

SUCCESS STORY
IN NIGERIA

On July 20, 2014, a man traveled by airplane to Lagos, Nigeria—
Africa's largest city. The man was infected with Ebola and died
in a Nigerian hospital five days later. He was the country's first
Ebola patient. He set off a chain of infection that resulted in 19
cases and seven deaths. WHO guidelines indicate the end of an
outbreak can be declared when 42 days have passed with no new
cases.[7] On October 20, Nigeria was declared Ebola free.

Nigeria has a population of approximately 170 million, which is
almost seven times the population of Guinea, Liberia, and Sierra
Leone combined.[8] Limiting the cases of Ebola in Nigeria and
preventing a potential epidemic is a remarkable success story.
The credit goes to strong leadership and a quick response by the
Nigerian government.

As soon as the first Ebola case was confirmed, Nigerian health
officials established an emergency operations center. With the
help of international organizations, they tracked all contacts of
the infected patient. They isolated people who were at risk of

Nigerian health officials screened people using infrared thermometers before allowing them to board flights.

developing the disease and provided treatment for those who became ill.

The Nigerian government began public awareness campaigns to educate people about the dangers of Ebola. Government officials enlisted the help of religious and community leaders to gain public cooperation. These efforts not only provided a successful outcome but also proved an Ebola outbreak can be controlled.

TRACING
THE HISTORY
OF A VIRUS

T he history of the Ebola virus dates back to the 1970s. In mid-September 1976, a small mission hospital in the central African nation of Zaire, now called the Democratic Republic of the Congo, reported two dozen cases of a mysterious illness. Fourteen patients died, and the mission's doctor alerted health department authorities in Kinshasa, Zaire's capital. The source of the disease was unknown, but the illness was spreading rapidly.

Blood samples from the victims were sent to overseas laboratories where experts could identify the

The miniscule Ebola virus spread disease, panic, and fear across the globe in 2014.

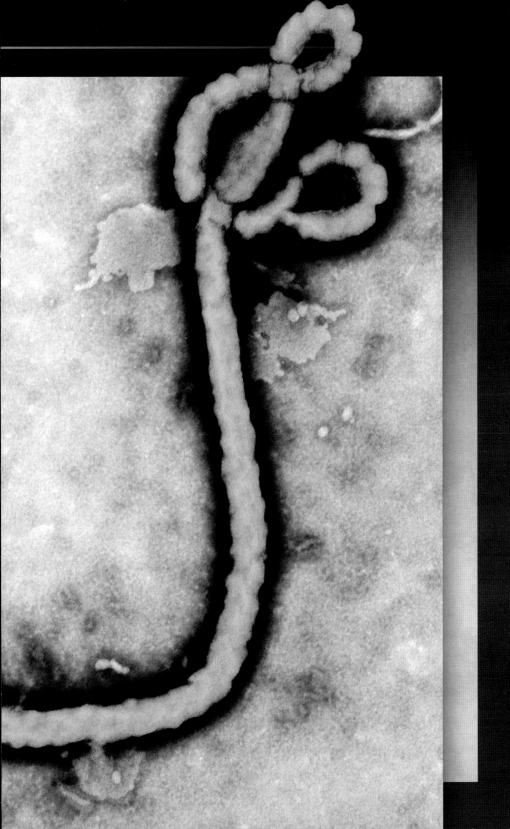

virus causing the illness. Scientist Peter Piot tested a blood sample at his laboratory in Antwerp, Belgium. When Piot viewed the cells under a microscope, he was surprised by what he saw. He recognized the sample as a filovirus—a disease that causes severe damage to the body and often results in death. However, this was different from any virus he had seen before.

Piot consulted other experts around the world who also studied the Zaire samples. They confirmed the illness had not been caused by any known virus—this was something new. Frederick Murphy, an expert from the US Centers for Disease Control and Prevention (CDC), reported, "This is the weirdest virus we have ever seen."[1] In October, Piot was part of an international team of scientists

FILOVIRUS FACTS

Filoviruses can cause severe illnesses that affect multiple organs and body systems in humans, monkeys, and apes. So far, only two filoviruses have been identified—Marburg and Ebola. The two viruses have some similarities. Both are transmitted from animals to humans, and both are spread from person to person through contact with bodily fluids.

Marburg virus was discovered in 1967 when laboratory workers developed a life-threatening disease after handling tissues from monkeys. The virus was named after Marburg, Germany, one of two sites of the outbreaks. These outbreaks resulted in seven deaths. Marburg emerged again in 1975 in South Africa, and a few cases have occurred since then.

Several strains of Ebola virus have been identified: Zaire, Sudan, Bundibugyo, Tai Forest, and Reston. The viruses are named after the sites where outbreaks first occurred.

and doctors that traveled to Zaire to investigate the cause of the illness.

TRACKING AN EPIDEMIC

The team of experts included members from France, Canada, South Africa, and the United States. Their journey was an adventure that involved flying to Kinshasa, taking a small transport aircraft to the Congo River port town of Bumba, and finally going on a rugged overland ride to the remote rain forest village of Yambuku. The natural beauty of the area contrasted with the horror of the new disease that was claiming the lives of its people.

The team visited the mission hospital. There, people from surrounding villages, as well as the doctors and nurses who cared for them, had become ill. Their symptoms included high fever, headache, vomiting, diarrhea, and excessive bleeding, which usually resulted in death.

"THE CHURCH AND THE RED ROOFS OF THE YAMBUKU MISSION APPEARED, LIKE MIRAGES, IN THE BLINDING SUNLIGHT. SURROUNDED BY A NEATLY SWEPT COURTYARD LINED WITH ROYAL PALM TREES AND IMMACULATE LAWNS, THEY SEEMED SURREAL. IT WAS DIFFICULT TO BELIEVE THAT THIS CLEAN, ORDERLY . . . PLACE WAS REALLY . . . THE HEART OF THE MYSTERIOUS KILLER VIRUS."[2]

—PETER PIOT

The hospital had closed because most of the staff had died. The team toured nearby villages, taking blood samples and gathering information about the number of cases and deaths.

FINDING ANSWERS

The scientists knew the reservoir host, or the source of the virus, was likely an animal. Similar viruses had been known to travel from animals to people. Still, the possibilities seemed endless. A person might have touched something bloody, such as the fresh meat of an infected monkey or antelope. Perhaps a person had been stung by an infected insect or bitten by an infected spider. Such blood-to-blood contact would have allowed the virus to pass to humans.

Identifying the source of the virus was important. However, it was not nearly as urgent as finding out how the virus was spreading from person to person. Like detectives unraveling a mystery, the doctors and scientists began asking questions. When did each person begin showing symptoms? Where did each of the sick people come from? Did the sick people have anything in common?

International scientists arrived in Zaire in late 1976 to study the mysterious new virus.

Some patterns began to emerge from this questioning. The team discovered most of the infected people came from areas served by the mission hospital. Many of the women who caught the virus had attended a clinic at the hospital where they received an injection as part of their prenatal care. Other people became ill after attending funerals of those who had died from the disease.

This evidence led the scientists to conclude the virus was spread through direct contact with the bodily fluids of someone who was ill with the virus. The needles used for injections at the hospital were reused without being properly sterilized. So if one person was infected, the virus spread to others who were injected with the same needle. People who cared for the sick and people who washed or prepared bodies for funerals came in contact with blood or vomit from a person who had

"AT THE BEGINNING OF EACH DAY, THE NUNS AT YAMBUKU HOSPITAL WOULD LAY OUT FIVE HYPODERMIC SYRINGES ON A TABLE AND THEY WOULD USE THEM TO GIVE SHOTS TO PATIENTS ALL DAY LONG . . . THEY PROCEEDED FROM SHOT TO SHOT WITHOUT RINSING THE NEEDLE, MOVING FROM ARM TO ARM, MIXING BLOOD WITH BLOOD."[3]

—AUTHOR RICHARD PRESTON

MORE TO THE
STORY

SUDAN OUTBREAK

In June 1976, a cotton factory worker in Sudan became ill with a fever, headache, and chest pains. The symptoms progressed to vomiting, diarrhea, and excessive bleeding. The man died a few days later. Soon the man's brother, who had taken care of him, and some of his coworkers at the cotton factory became ill. The brother recovered from the illness, but most of the others died. The disease spread rapidly, eventually reaching a hospital in a nearby town where many patients and staff became infected.

Between June and November, more than 280 cases were recorded in Sudan, with a death rate higher than 50 percent.[4] Then, for unknown reasons, the virus disappeared. It may have killed people so quickly they did not have time to infect others.

The Zaire outbreak happened a few months later. People wondered if there was a link between these events. Although there was extensive trade between the two areas, no direct connection was identified. The Zaire strain of the virus is different from the Sudan strain. Although the Sudan outbreak happened first, the Zaire outbreak led to the identification and naming of the Ebola virus.

the virus. The caregivers soon exhibited symptoms of the illness.

STOPPING THE EPIDEMIC

The source of the virus remained a mystery, but the doctors knew the spread of the epidemic could be controlled. The key was education. Epidemiologists went from village to village and isolated anyone who was sick or who had come into direct contact with the virus. They made sure the community had necessary information about basic hygiene. The nameless epidemic eventually came to an end after taking the lives of approximately 300 people.[5]

The team of scientists and doctors did not want to name the virus Yambuku, after the village where it had originated. They felt doing so would forever link the name of the village with the deadly illness. Instead, they decided to name the virus after a river in the region. Upon consulting a map of Zaire, they chose the name that would come to represent one of the world's deadliest and most feared diseases—Ebola.

During the 1976 outbreak, doctors developed the equipment and procedures they would need to protect themselves from the virus.

EBOLA RESTON

In 1989, dozens of laboratory monkeys died at a research center in Reston, Virginia—a short distance from the US capital, Washington, DC. A team of US Army scientists was called in to investigate the cause of the animals' deaths.

The events unfolded like the plot of a horror story. Scientists had to prevent the spread of the disease without alerting the public to the presence of a deadly virus in their midst. They discovered the virus was not Ebola Zaire but rather a different strain, which they named Ebola Reston. Although Ebola Reston is deadly to monkeys, it does not affect humans.

The story of the Ebola outbreak in Reston did not become widely known until it was revealed in author Richard Preston's nonfiction thriller *The Hot Zone*. The book raised public awareness of Ebola and alerted people to the challenges of controlling deadly diseases.

HISTORY OF EBOLA OUTBREAKS

Between 1976 and 2012, more than 20 Ebola outbreaks occurred in African countries. The specific strain of Ebola virus differed between outbreaks, but all were closely related. The duration and severity of these incidents varied widely. The number of cases ranged from 1 to 425, and the death rate was as low as 0 percent and as high as 100 percent.[6] Major outbreaks appeared in 1995 and 2007 in the Democratic Republic of the Congo and in 2000 in Uganda. The numbers of cases and deaths measured in the hundreds.

The number of deaths in the 2014 outbreak eventually outnumbered the total deaths in all previous outbreaks combined. Why did the 2014 Ebola epidemic spiral out of control? One factor was the population density in the affected areas. A combination of other factors also contributed to history's worst Ebola outbreak. Among them were insufficient health systems and resources in West Africa and a lack of understanding and cooperation among the people living there. One of the most serious problems was the delayed response from the international community after the outbreak began.

In an interview in September 2014, Piot said, "The longer we wait, the longer there is an insufficient response, the worse it will get, the more difficult it will be to control this epidemic through . . . all the methods that worked in the past."[7]

VIRUS DETECTIVE

As a young boy growing up in Belgium, Peter Piot rode his bicycle to a local museum. He was fascinated by pictures of people suffering from a disease called leprosy and stories about a man who worked with them. This experience sparked Piot's interest in medicine and his desire to help people.

By the age of 27, Piot had a medical degree and was working as a microbiologist—a scientist who studies viruses and other microscopic organisms. His trip to Zaire in 1976 was the first of many battles he waged against infectious diseases in Africa and elsewhere. He devoted much of his career to fighting acquired immune deficiency syndrome (AIDS). He was the founding director of UNAIDS, an international program to promote worldwide action to prevent the spread of the disease. In 2010, Piot became director of the London School of Hygiene and Tropical Medicine, where he continued to lead research on global health issues.

CHAPTER THREE

RESPONDING
TO THE CRISIS

The Ebola epidemic in West Africa was identified in March 2014, but local governments failed to control the spread of the disease. Critics argue government leaders did not properly respond to the outbreak until it threatened major cities, such as Monrovia, Liberia. By the time the government took action, designated treatment centers and ambulance services were overwhelmed. Other people agree regional health systems were unprepared, while some believe leaders did the best they could under the circumstances.

Critics blamed Liberian president Ellen Johnson Sirleaf and other government officials for the slow initial response to the outbreak.

FIRST RESPONDERS

Doctors Without Borders is a medical group that responds to emergencies around the world. The organization was established in France, so it is often called by its French name—Médecins Sans Frontières (MSF). This group was among the first to send help to West Africa in March 2014. MSF set up isolation wards for Ebola patients in Guinea and provided medical support in Liberia and Sierra Leone as the deadly virus spread to those countries. By August, the director of MSF, Bart Janssens, made a desperate public plea to countries around the world for medical experts and resources to help fight the epidemic. "All our Ebola experts are mobilized," he stated. "We simply cannot do more."[1]

Samaritan's Purse is a religious charity that responded to the Ebola crisis in Liberia in

"THIS LARGE EBOLA OUTBREAK COULD HAVE BEEN PREVENTED WITH AN EFFECTIVE PUBLIC HEALTH RESPONSE AT THE BEGINNING. BUT THE WEAK HEALTH SYSTEMS OF THE AFFECTED COUNTRIES LEFT THEM UNPREPARED TO RESPOND TO THE OUTBREAK. THE INTERNATIONAL COMMUNITY SHOULD HAVE BEEN MORE GENEROUS IN SUPPORTING POORER COUNTRIES SO THEY COULD DEVELOP THE RESPONSE CAPACITIES NEEDED TO CONTAIN THE OUTBREAK."[2]

—LAWRENCE GOSTIN, LAW PROFESSOR, GEORGETOWN UNIVERSITY

March 2014. The organization began a national awareness campaign to educate local people about hygiene and disease prevention. In cooperation with Liberia's Ministry of Health and other health groups, Samaritan's Purse provided care for Ebola patients in hospitals and clinics throughout Liberia.

MSF established its own Ebola treatment facilities in the affected areas.

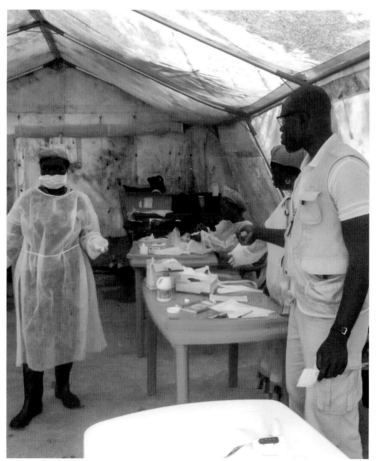

EBOLA WAR ROOM

Pardis Sabeti is head of a laboratory at Harvard University, where she specializes in studying the way viruses change over time. In May 2014, she set up what became known as the Ebola war room. Over a period of several months, Sabeti and a team of scientists met regularly in the war room to plan a defense against Ebola. Their work centered on studying blood samples from Ebola victims in Sierra Leone in order to develop drugs to combat the disease.

Sabeti's group did not find a way to treat Ebola, but the results of the study were valuable. They proved Ebola was not being spread through repeated contact with infected animals. Instead, it was being spread from person to person. This information allowed researchers to narrow their focus on how to stop the spread of the disease.

The WHO is the part of the United Nations responsible for providing leadership on global health matters. In March 2014, it distributed medical supplies and protection materials in Guinea and worked with local health officials to mobilize a response to the Ebola outbreak. Critics later blamed the WHO for the delay in alerting the global community to the seriousness of the epidemic.

On August 8, 2014, the WHO declared the Ebola epidemic "a public health emergency of international concern."[3] Under the International Health Regulations—a set of procedures to protect public health—such an emergency may require a coordinated international response. Within the following few weeks, the United States, the United Kingdom, Cuba, France, and China pledged aid to West Africa.

WAKING UP THE WORLD

In September 2014, the United Nations held a meeting regarding the health crisis in West Africa. Doctors from the area delivered the disturbing report that infection rates were doubling every three weeks. They described the collapse of public health systems in the area and the panic of desperate people seeking treatment. Joanne Liu, president of MSF, described the situation in Monrovia, where the hospitals were filled to capacity: "The sick continue to be turned away, only to return home and spread the virus among loved ones and neighbors. The isolation centers . . . must be established now."[4] Her message was clear. The world was doing too little and moving too slowly.

In an address to the meeting, US president Barack Obama urged other world leaders to join the United States in providing medical services and equipment. "We are not moving fast enough. We are not doing enough," the president said. "There is still a significant gap between where we are and where we need to be."[5]

UNDERSTANDING THE GAP

On September 19, the United Nations formed an emergency task force and appealed to member nations for approximately $1 billion to fight the Ebola epidemic. The United States promised to send 3,000 troops to build treatment centers and $500 million to support the effort.[6] Although many countries responded generously, the disease was spreading faster than help could arrive.

At that time, the affected countries needed approximately three times more beds for patients and twice as many dead-body management teams. They also

US president Barack Obama pledged US assistance to Ebola-affected areas and asked that other nations join in aiding the effort.

needed more health experts who had experience dealing with Ebola and setting up treatment centers. They needed laboratories to test patients who had not yet been confirmed as Ebola victims. By September, less than $350 million had actually been donated, and only a few countries had sent doctors to the region.[7] Additional treatment centers would be useless without people to run them.

Regarding the urgent needs in Guinea, Liberia, and Sierra Leone, one journalist wrote, "They do not need novice do-gooders from the wealthy world, but people experienced in working under the stifling conditions of tropical heat, the desperation of supplies deficits, and the fearfulness of epidemics."[8] The problem was a lack of people with those qualifications.

HOME CARE KITS

Plastic buckets filled with simple household items and protective gear represented an attempt to bridge the gap between available care and what was needed in the hot zones. Thousands of these so-called home care kits were distributed in Liberia. Each bucket contained gloves, masks, disposable gowns, chlorine powder, soap, a spray bottle, and plastic bags.

Health officials provided instruction for the use of the kits. Sometimes they went door-to-door to ensure families knew how to use the materials to care for an Ebola patient at home. Training included the importance of wearing personal protection, how to mix chlorine powder and water in a spray bottle to make a disinfecting solution, and how to properly dispose of infected items in plastic bags. Experts hoped even the minimal protection provided by the home care kits might help break the cycle of transmission.

FROM THE HEADLINES

THE FATE OF EBOLA TREATMENT CENTERS

In September 2014, President Obama announced plans to send 3,000 troops to West Africa to build 17 Ebola treatment centers.[9] At that time, Ebola patients were being turned away because existing facilities had no beds for them.

Among the soldiers who traveled to Liberia was 20-year-old Joshua Gilbertson, a member of the US Army Engineer Brigade. Gilbertson told reporters about his experiences traveling through the jungle to survey sites for treatment centers and then creating models and blueprints for building them. "Due to the remoteness and lack of proper roads to a couple locations, we often flew by helicopter to save time," he said. "The Ebola facilities were all strategically placed throughout the country to give reasonably close medical care for any and all possible Ebola cases."[10]

US soldiers worked with local soldiers and contractors to construct the treatment centers. By mid-December, many of the new treatment centers had been built, but there were not enough patients to fill them. Several of the US-built facilities never treated a single Ebola patient.

The construction effort continued even as the epidemic faded in the late fall. Two of the planned centers were canceled as a result of the reduced demand. Many criticized the waste of

US Army troops built treatment centers in preparation for a predicted worst-case scenario involving more than 1 million Ebola victims. The epidemic ended up being much less severe.

money on buildings that served no purpose. Others warned the disease could flare up again and it was better to be prepared for the worst.

Relatively few doctors and nurses outside of Africa had experience with Ebola virus disease. Health workers in the affected countries often lacked proper training in how to protect themselves and others. Therefore, the most urgent needs included education and training for health-care workers.

Health-care workers were not the only people who needed education. The spread of the disease worsened because many people in the Ebola-affected countries did not realize the danger. They did not understand why sick family members were kept isolated or why doctors would not let them see or touch loved ones at a funeral.

MAKING PROGRESS?

Despite the delay in response and the overwhelming nature of the needs in West Africa, local efforts and international support seemed to make a difference. The United Nations established the 70-70-60 plan. The goal of the plan was to get 70 percent of the cases isolated and treated and 70 percent of the deceased safely buried within the 60 days between October 1 and December 1, 2014.[11] The goals for safe burials were met in Liberia,

Guinea, and Sierra Leone. The goals for isolation were met in all but Sierra Leone.

Working with the governments of France, the United Kingdom, and the United States, the WHO coordinated training for doctors and other health-care workers. It set up community education programs in West Africa. The rate of new cases declined slightly, but the progress was short-lived. Experts warned the Ebola response had to be more than a short-term intensive effort. Health systems were collapsing, and long-term international support was needed not only to maintain progress but also to prevent future crises.

Additional concerns arose over the number of health-care workers who had become ill with Ebola.

RESPECTING CULTURAL TRADITIONS

In West Africa, burial traditions contributed to Ebola's spread. A person's body is most contagious right after he or she dies. Some burial practices involved washing or touching the body of the deceased person. Sometimes the deceased person's belongings, which might have been infected, were distributed to family members or friends. People often became ill after attending the funeral of someone who died from Ebola.

Burial practices are an important part of people's culture. The challenge for health authorities was to provide alternative practices that would prevent the spread of Ebola while still respecting traditions. A team of experts that included religious leaders developed safe and dignified burial procedures that honored the deceased person as well as the grieving family and friends.

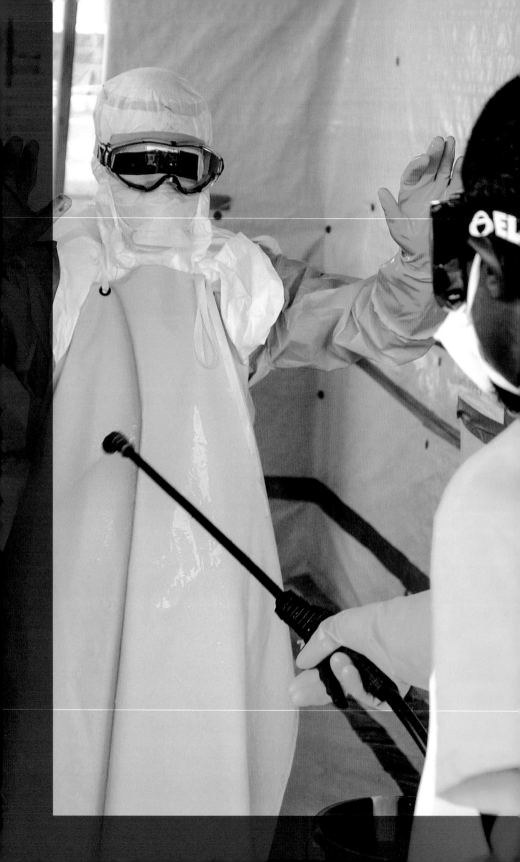

By November 2014, more than 300 medical workers in West Africa had died from the disease.[12] Their deaths were mainly due to shortages or improper use of protective equipment. Several health-care workers from other countries, including the United States and European nations, had become infected with the disease. They were flown back to their home countries for treatment. The Ebola epidemic was becoming a global threat.

CUBA'S CONTRIBUTION

Cuba does not rank among the world's largest countries in size, population, or wealth. But it was the first country to dedicate hundreds of health-care workers to the Ebola crisis in West Africa.

When Cuban doctors graduate from medical school, they often make a commitment to serve a cause, such as fighting an epidemic or helping in a natural disaster. They receive training for the specific disease they will be treating, and they study the region's culture and history.

Medical workers dealing with Ebola must take extreme measures to avoid being infected with the disease themselves.

CHAPTER FOUR

A GLOBAL
THREAT

On July 20, 2014, Patrick Sawyer boarded an airplane in Liberia, where he worked as an economic consultant. He flew to Lagos, Nigeria, to attend a conference. Although Sawyer did not appear to be ill when he left Liberia, he collapsed at the Lagos airport. He was taken to a hospital where he was diagnosed with Ebola and died five days later.

Sawyer was originally from Nigeria, but he moved to the United States and became a US citizen. His wife and three children lived in Minnesota, where Sawyer planned to return within the next month. His case emphasized the fact that Ebola was just a plane ride away from any country on Earth.

The bustling city of Lagos, Nigeria, braced for a potential outbreak after an Ebola patient died there in July 2014.

BRINGING PATIENTS HOME

In Patrick Sawyer's case, a plane ride exposed many other people to a deadly disease. Although quick action by Nigerian health authorities prevented a serious outbreak, seven people died. Similar cases involved US medical workers Dr. Kent Brantly and Nancy Writebol.

On July 23, 2014, Brantly, a US medical missionary working at an Ebola treatment center in Liberia, awoke feeling ill. Only three days before, Brantly had sent his family back to Texas to attend a wedding. He planned to join them a week later. Within a few days, however, he was diagnosed with Ebola virus disease. At about the same time, Nancy Writebol, a US nurse at the same clinic, was also diagnosed. It was later determined both Brantly and Writebol may have been infected by a Liberian health-care worker who had caught the disease from a patient.

A decision was made to send Brantly and Writebol home to the United States for treatment. The plane used to transport each patient was a modified jet. It was fitted with an isolation chamber and a foam cot. Medical equipment monitored blood pressure and administered oxygen and fluids to keep the patient comfortable. A highly trained medical crew accompanied each patient on the 14-hour trip.

Near death on August 2, Brantly was flown to Emory University Hospital in Atlanta, Georgia, for treatment. Three days later, Writebol was

THE GRAY BIRD

The plane used to transport Ebola patients Kent Brantly and Nancy Writebol to the United States was called the Gray Bird. It was one of three business jets once owned by the Danish Air Force and was originally modified for maritime missions around Greenland.

In 2005, Phoenix Air, an air ambulance service in the state of Georgia, bought the planes. Phoenix Air worked with the CDC to modify the planes to transport patients with infectious diseases. A thick, clear, plastic tent and filtered air supply were designed to keep the cabin clear of infections.

The modifications made the Gray Bird perfect for transporting Ebola patients. After the successful missions from West Africa to the United States, the plane returned to Georgia. There, the plastic tent was removed, loaded into a medical waste bag, and safely destroyed. The cabin was sprayed with disinfectant, and the plane was ready for future missions.

Doctors took heavy precautions while transporting
Writebol to a US hospital.

transported to the same hospital. By August 21, both

Brantly and Writebol had recovered from the virus and

were released from the hospital.

Before leaving Liberia, Brantly and Writebol had

received an experimental drug called ZMapp. It is

unknown whether the drug helped them or they

improved on their own. The same drug had been given to

a Spanish Ebola patient, but he did not survive.

EBOLA IN THE UNITED STATES

Brantly and Writebol were American Ebola patients, but they had contracted the virus in West Africa. The disease, in the minds of many Americans, remained a distant threat. That idea quickly changed in September 2014.

Thomas Eric Duncan lived in a rented room in Monrovia, Liberia. On September 15, he helped his landlord's daughter, who was ill with Ebola, get to a hospital. When she was turned away for lack of space, Duncan carried the woman back to her home. A few days later, Duncan set out on a trip to the United States to visit family and friends. He flew from Liberia to Brussels, Belgium, then to Washington, DC. He finally arrived in Dallas, Texas, on September 20. He did not appear ill during the trip.

A THREAT TO NATIONAL SECURITY

President Obama called Ebola "a national security priority."[1] He sent US troops to West Africa to help prevent the spread of the disease. He warned the disease could pose a danger to the United States.

The president's warning was taken seriously. The CDC set up an emergency operations center to handle calls from hospitals around the country seeking advice on potential Ebola cases. CDC leaders met daily with government officials to monitor progress and plan effective action against the spread of the disease.

On September 24, Duncan began to have a fever, headache, and stomach pain. He visited the emergency room of a hospital in Dallas, but he was sent home without being tested for Ebola. By September 28, his condition was much worse, and he was rushed back to the hospital in an ambulance. Duncan was diagnosed with Ebola virus disease and put in isolation, where he died on October 8.

Thomas Eric Duncan was the first person diagnosed with Ebola virus disease in the United States. Officials from the CDC traced anyone who had potentially come into contact with him. People who may have been exposed to the virus were monitored for 21 days. Although the risk of

LEGAL ISSUES

Despite his symptoms and the fact he had traveled from Liberia, Thomas Eric Duncan was not tested for Ebola when he first visited the emergency room at a Dallas hospital. Failure to recognize the potential seriousness of Duncan's condition, which resulted in his death a few days later, raised legal issues for the hospital. Members of Duncan's family questioned whether prompt treatment when Duncan first visited the hospital might have saved his life.

Two of the nurses who treated Duncan contracted Ebola. They later recovered, but their cases raised questions about the hospital where Duncan was treated. Observers wondered if the hospital had proper procedures in place to protect staff against Ebola.

In a settlement with Duncan's family, the hospital covered the expenses of Duncan's care and paid an undisclosed sum of money. It also increased safety precautions for staff treating potential Ebola patients.

After Duncan was diagnosed with Ebola, teams were sent to sanitize the apartment where he had been staying.

the virus spreading was limited, the fear of catching Ebola had already spread. The disease was no longer seen as a distant threat, and some people began to panic. Despite campaigns to educate the public about Ebola, myths and misunderstandings thrived.

FROM THE HEADLINES

THE SPREAD OF EBOLA

Between August and December 2014, at least 24 Ebola patients were treated in the United States and Europe. They included health-care workers, missionaries, aid workers, and a television news cameraman who caught the disease in West Africa. The patients were transported back to their home countries for treatment. One nurse in Spain was diagnosed with Ebola after treating patients who returned from West Africa with the virus. All but five of the Ebola patients who received treatment outside of Africa survived the disease.

Between April and November 2014, more than 500 health-care workers became infected with Ebola and were treated in West Africa. More than 300 of them died.[2] What accounted for the dramatic difference in survival rates? Health-care facilities in the United States and Europe were much better equipped than those in West Africa. Medical staff with adequate personal protective equipment could effectively isolate patients and monitor them around the clock. Routine medications, often in short supply in West African clinics, kept patients comfortable and stable while their bodies fought the disease. In addition, US patients had access to some experimental drugs that were not available elsewhere.

EBOLA CASE COUNTS AS OF JULY 2015

COUNTRY	TOTAL CASES	DEATHS
Sierra Leone	13,250	3,949
Liberia	10,666	4,806
Guinea	3,783	2,512
Nigeria	20	8
Mali	8	6
United States	4	1
Italy	1	0
Senegal	1	0
Spain	1	0
United Kingdom	1	0[3]

CHAPTER FIVE

JUST THE FACTS,
PLEASE

The Ebola virus causes a serious disease that is often fatal, but in 2014 fear of the disease spread more quickly than the virus itself. People became concerned they could catch Ebola by being in the same room with someone who had the disease even though that person did not show any symptoms. They believed anyone who had Ebola would die. They feared Ebola was easy to catch and an Ebola epidemic was unstoppable. All these assumptions were incorrect.

THE TRUTH ABOUT EBOLA

The Ebola virus is transmitted to humans by wild animals found in Africa, and the virus is spread through human-to-human contact. The Ebola virus is spread

Fears about Ebola led some protesters to call for a ban on all flights from West Africa to the United States.

only through direct contact with the bodily fluids—such as blood, sweat, vomit, or saliva—of someone who is ill with the virus. A person who has the virus cannot spread the disease until he or she has symptoms of the illness, so the disease cannot be caught from someone who does not appear to be sick.

DO MOSQUITOS SPREAD EBOLA?

Because Africa has many mosquitoes, and because mosquitoes spread many diseases, mosquitoes might seem to be likely hosts of the Ebola virus. But they are not. Mosquitoes do not fly from person to person, biting one after another. Even if a mosquito bit a person with Ebola, the mosquito would not transmit the infected person's blood to another person.

Only female mosquitoes bite, and they need blood only when they are ready to lay eggs. After taking in blood, the mosquito rests for a period of time to digest the blood so it can nourish its eggs. Then it seeks water in which to lay the eggs. When a mosquito bites, it injects saliva into a person. Ebola cannot get into mosquito saliva, so there is no danger of getting the Ebola virus from a mosquito bite.

Although the Ebola virus is often fatal, catching Ebola is not an automatic death sentence. Many patients survive. The survival rate depends on the kind of Ebola virus the person has and the medical care the person receives. There is no cure for Ebola, but if a patient can be kept alive by treating the symptoms, his or her body can fight the disease.

Ebola can spread rapidly through a population, but doctors emphasize Ebola is very hard to catch. Wearing protective clothing and practicing careful hygiene when caring for Ebola patients can slow the spread of the disease.

SYMPTOMS OF EBOLA

The length of time between infection with a virus and the appearance of symptoms is known as the incubation period. For Ebola virus disease, the incubation period can range from 2 to 21 days. The first symptoms are usually fatigue, headache, and a sudden fever. Many patients also suffer from muscle pain and a sore throat. Vomiting, diarrhea, and rashes follow. In the later stages of the disease, some victims suffer from internal and external

Ebola victims are buried rapidly and carefully to prevent contact with bodily fluids.

DIAGNOSING EBOLA

Diagnosis of Ebola during the outbreak was difficult because its early symptoms—fever, headache, and fatigue—can indicate many different diseases. If a person with those symptoms is known to have contacted an Ebola patient or an animal that could have been infected with Ebola, serious precautions are necessary.

A person suspected of having Ebola is isolated and has blood samples taken and tested. During the Ebola epidemic of 2014, no rapid test for diagnosing the disease was available. It took several days after symptoms started for the virus to be detected in the blood. Therefore, any person suspected of having Ebola was kept away from others and monitored to make sure he or she was free of the disease.

bleeding. Patients who die generally succumb to organ failure and shock.

People with Ebola virus disease are not contagious until they develop symptoms. They remain contagious as long as their blood and other bodily fluids contain the virus. This is why blood tests are necessary to determine if a patient has recovered from the disease.

SEEKING THE SOURCE

The search for Ebola's reservoir host began during the Zaire outbreak in 1976. Researchers in Africa tested bedbugs, pigs, rodents, squirrels, and monkeys. No evidence of the virus was found in any of them. Over the next 20 years, research continued without success. However, scientists narrowed the search. It was clear the reservoir host was a forest mammal and did not have frequent contact with people.

Between 2001 and 2003, scientists tested more than 1,000 animals in areas of Africa that had suffered Ebola outbreaks.[1] This research identified fruit bats as likely reservoirs of the virus. The question of how the virus spread from bats to humans remained unanswered. That spillover may have occurred directly if, for example, people ate the meat of infected bats. Or it may have occurred indirectly if people came into contact with other animals that had been infected by the bats.

SEPARATING FACT FROM FICTION

Based on the growing crisis in West Africa, many people assumed an Ebola epidemic was unstoppable. The fear was understandable, but the assumption was not true. The spread of Ebola can be stopped by isolating those who are sick, finding and monitoring all people who have been exposed to the virus, and safely burying anyone who has died from the virus. Successful Ebola responses in Nigeria, Senegal, and Mali proved the disease could be controlled. Each of those countries limited the spread of Ebola by

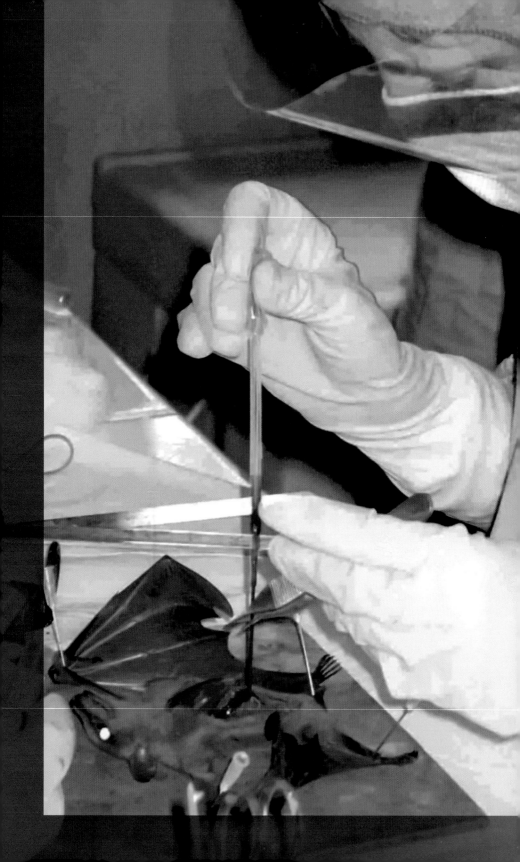

identifying the disease, tracing contacts, setting up emergency centers, and informing the public. By January 2015, all three countries had been declared Ebola free.

The countries in West Africa at the center of the 2014 outbreak did not have the resources to put such procedures in place. In countries with better procedures and facilities, the spread of the virus was effectively stopped.

Another widespread myth about Ebola was the belief a cure or a vaccine existed. Although many scientists and drug companies throughout the world were working to develop medicines and vaccines to treat and prevent Ebola, none had proven effective. Many months of testing would be necessary before they could be used by the public.

Extensive testing revealed bats were the likely source of the Ebola virus.

CHAPTER SIX

THERE IS
NO CURE

E bola virus disease was discovered in 1976, but decades later there was still no cure. The scale of the 2014 epidemic in West Africa focused worldwide attention on the disease, but prior to that, it received little notice. The populations affected by earlier Ebola outbreaks were relatively small compared with those affected by other diseases, such as AIDS. Researchers and drug companies focused on developing cures for more common diseases.

By the time of the 2014 outbreak, a few drugs were in development, but they were not ready for use on humans. In the United States, drugs must be approved by the Food and Drug Administration (FDA), the government agency that oversees drug safety. The FDA

When studying Ebola, researchers are required to observe the CDC's strictest safety procedures.

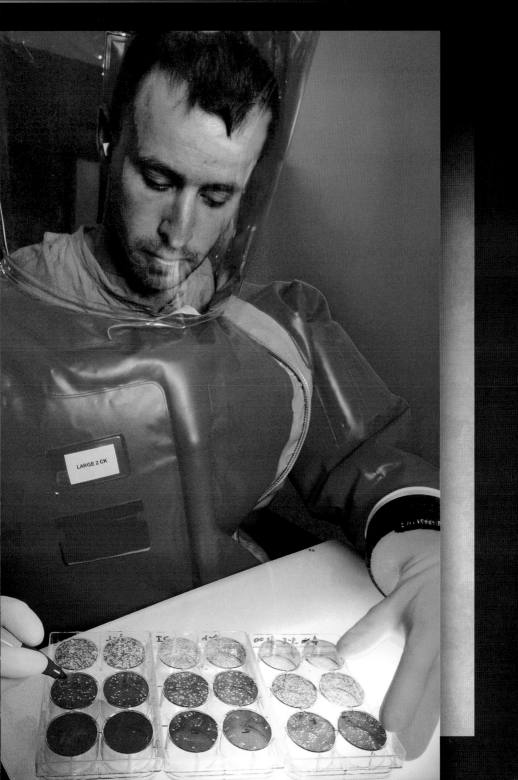

requires three phases of extensive testing on thousands of people. The process is very expensive and can take several years.

A PROMISING DRUG

The experimental drug known as ZMapp seemed to hold the most promise as a possible treatment for Ebola virus disease. Researchers had been investigating different combinations of antibodies, parts of the immune system that help fight disease. ZMapp was comprised of three antibodies that could be injected into a patient's bloodstream. The drug was tested on 18 monkeys infected with Ebola virus. Even though some of the monkeys were in the later stages of the disease, all of them survived.[1]

However, at the time of the Ebola epidemic, the drug was

DEVELOPING ZMAPP

Larry Zeitlin and Kevin Whaley worked together as research scientists in the 1990s. They focused on improving public health by developing drugs to treat destructive viruses. In 2003, they founded Mapp Biopharmaceutical Company in California.

With a staff of only nine people, Mapp worked to develop treatments for diseases not being addressed by larger companies. One of those diseases was Ebola. Because Ebola virus was relatively unknown and previous outbreaks had been controlled, there was very little funding for research. The development of ZMapp represented years of dedicated work. The company's vision paid off when two Ebola patients seemed to make progress after receiving ZMapp in July 2014.

still untested on humans. Researchers were cautious about predicting the effectiveness of a drug for humans based only on animal testing.

WHO SHOULD GET THE DRUG?

In late July 2014, the limited doses of ZMapp that were available in Sierra Leone were given to Brantly and Writebol. The drug appeared to help, and within a few days, Brantly and Writebol were flown to the United States for further treatment. Both recovered completely.

Because hundreds of African Ebola patients were dying, some people criticized the decision to give the scarce supply of the experimental drug to two white Americans. Others pointed out the Americans served as guinea pigs for the untested drug. Experts said it was too soon to conclude whether the drug had been responsible for their recovery.

DEVELOPING A VACCINE

While drug companies scrambled to ramp up production of ZMapp and other possible treatments for Ebola, other researchers focused on developing a vaccine to prevent

The Ebola vaccine continued to undergo testing and further study in early 2015.

the disease. A vaccine stimulates the immune system
to help it defend against future exposure to a disease.
An experimental Ebola vaccine was tried out on healthy
volunteers, and the results were good. Blood tests showed
the vaccine helped their bodies produce antibodies
against Ebola virus disease.

Large-scale testing was still needed before the vaccine
could be approved. One method of testing would involve

giving the vaccine to half of the participants in the test group, giving a placebo to the other half, and then comparing the results. Health officials argued it would be unfair to the group that did not receive the vaccine. If the vaccine worked, the placebo group would not be protected. Another method of testing would involve giving all the participants the vaccine but at different times.

Until drugs and vaccines could be tested and approved for widespread use against Ebola—a process that could take a significant amount of time—the primary tools to fight the disease remained isolation and monitoring. These procedures were difficult to enforce in Africa, and they caused controversy in the United States.

PHARMING

ZMapp seemed to be the most promising treatment for Ebola, but the limited supply was soon used up. To provide additional quantities of ZMapp, scientists used a process called "pharming," which means modifying plants to produce pharmaceuticals, or medically useful products. Pharming was developed in the 1980s, and it has become an efficient way to manufacture drugs. It is quicker and less expensive than using laboratory animals.

In the case of ZMapp, tobacco plants raised in Kentucky greenhouses were submerged in a solution with a modified plant virus. The virus caused the plants to produce the antibodies in ZMapp. The process took approximately a week. The tobacco leaves were harvested, and the antibodies were purified, tested, and formulated into the drug.

CHAPTER SEVEN

QUARANTINE
CONTROVERSY

D r. Craig Spencer returned to New York in October 2014 after spending five weeks in West Africa, where he treated Ebola patients. He had no symptoms of illness, but he monitored his temperature every day—a standard precaution taken by anyone who had been in West Africa in late 2014. Other than that, Spencer went about his regular life, which included riding the subway and going to a bowling alley and other public places.

On October 23, Spencer had a fever and went to Bellevue Hospital, where he was diagnosed with Ebola. He received treatment, recovered completely, and was released from the hospital on November 11. No one with whom Spencer came into contact became ill. Still,

Dr. Craig Spencer found himself at the center of a quarantine controversy in late 2014.

he was accused of irresponsible behavior for going out in public after he returned from West Africa. His case sparked a quarantine controversy.

MILITARY QUARANTINE

During the quarantine controversy, the US secretary of defense approved a policy for military personnel returning from West Africa. Troops who served in Ebola areas would be held in quarantine for 21 days. The quarantine would be enforced for all returning personnel, even if they had no symptoms and had not been in direct contact with Ebola patients in Africa.

Military officials said the policy reflected "an abundance of caution" in order to protect troops, their families, and the communities to which they returned.[1] Bases designated by each of the military services would be used to quarantine the troops.

Leaders of all branches of the armed forces further defended their policy by pointing out many of the US troops were inexperienced in medical issues. The officials expressed concern that, unlike health-care professionals, returning troops might not follow strict guidelines for self-monitoring. The troops would therefore be better protected in mandatory quarantine.

ISOLATION VERSUS QUARANTINE

The terms *isolation* and *quarantine* were sometimes used interchangeably during the Ebola crisis, but they mean very different things. Isolation refers to separating sick people from healthy people to stop the spread of a disease. In West Africa, isolation was a principal method for controlling Ebola, but it was very difficult to manage. Limited capacity in health-care facilities and an overwhelming number of Ebola patients made it almost impossible to isolate those who were sick. Family members sometimes did not understand why they could not touch or care for loved ones who were suffering from Ebola. In the United States, special Ebola treatment facilities were set up in hospitals in major cities. Although only a few Ebola cases were treated in the United States, no one questioned the need to isolate the patients.

Quarantine is a preventive measure. Healthy people who are at risk of developing an infectious disease are quarantined, or separated from others, to see if they become sick. This method lowers the risk of spreading a disease. During the Ebola crisis, there was a great deal of debate in the United States over who should be quarantined and how a quarantine should be enforced.

In West Africa, Ebola quarantines were strictly enforced, sometimes even using armed guards.

WHO IS IN CHARGE?

Who has the right to make quarantine rules? According to US law, the states have the right to enforce quarantines within their borders. However, the federal government can override the states if the quarantines are a national security issue. The US government was concerned with the safety of the public and the well-being of those who risked their lives caring for Ebola patients in West Africa. It set up its own response to the outbreak.

The federal government, the medical community, and the states seemed to have different opinions about quarantines, and their rules varied. The challenge was finding a way

HISTORY OF QUARANTINE

The use of quarantine to prevent the spread of disease is centuries old. During the Middle Ages, quarantine was used to protect cities from plague epidemics. Ships arriving from infected ports were required to anchor for 40 days before landing in Venice, Italy. The word *quarantine* comes from the Italian word for 40.

During the 1800s, state and local governments in the United States were responsible for enforcing quarantines. Outbreaks of cholera on ships arriving from Europe led to a federal role in quarantine activities. The US Public Health Service became responsible for preventing the spread of diseases from foreign countries into the United States.

In 1967, the responsibility for quarantine in the United States was transferred to the agency now known as the CDC. The CDC maintains 20 quarantine stations throughout the United States.[2] It provides federal guidelines for preventing the spread of disease.

to put proper safeguards in place without making public health concerns a major political issue.

DIFFERENT APPROACHES TO THE PROBLEM

The US Department of Homeland Security coordinated the response to prevent the spread of Ebola in the United States. Travelers entering the country from Guinea, Sierra Leone, or Liberia were routed through one of five airports equipped with enhanced passenger screening. The airports were located in New York, New York; Newark, New Jersey; Chicago, Illinois; Atlanta, Georgia; and Washington, DC. The enhanced screening consisted of identifying travelers from Ebola-affected countries and having them complete a questionnaire. Travelers who had been exposed to Ebola or who had a fever or other symptoms were given a health assessment. If necessary, travelers were taken to a hospital for further evaluation or referred to a local health department for monitoring.

The CDC issued federal guidelines for airline travelers from Ebola-affected nations who passed the enhanced screening procedures. They were required to self-monitor

MORE TO THE
STORY

WELCOME TO THE UNITED STATES

The CDC established a screening process for airline travelers arriving in the United States from Guinea, Sierra Leone, or Liberia. Upon arrival, each traveler was taken to a special screening area. Department of Homeland Security staff asked the traveler questions to determine possible risk of Ebola exposure. The staff member took the traveler's temperature and checked for other symptoms of Ebola. The traveler had to provide contact information so public health workers could follow up later.

Travelers who had a fever or other symptoms were required to undergo additional screening. Travelers who had no symptoms were issued a Check and Report Ebola kit. The kit included a digital thermometer, directions for reading the thermometer, a reminder to carry out the required health checks, a list of symptoms, and a list of health department telephone numbers. Travelers were instructed to take their temperature every morning and night for 21 days and to record each thermometer reading. They were told to call a health department or doctor to report a fever or any other symptoms.

Airport personnel around the world practiced procedures for dealing with incoming Ebola threats.

for 21 days and report the results to the CDC. If they failed to report, the agency would track them down.

The CDC also issued guidelines for doctors and other health-care professionals returning from West Africa after working with Ebola patients. The guidelines called for these individuals to monitor themselves for 21 days, but the CDC did not recommend quarantine. MSF issued similar guidelines for returning staff members, but the organization discouraged individuals from going to work during the 21-day period.

Several states issued rules much stricter than the federal guidelines. The governors of New York, New Jersey, and Illinois announced they would enforce mandatory home quarantines for all travelers entering their states who had contact with Ebola patients in West Africa. New York and New Jersey added the requirement of twice-daily monitoring by health officials.

THE ARGUMENT AGAINST QUARANTINE

Many doctors advised against mandatory quarantines, which they felt would have little benefit in preventing the spread of Ebola in the United States. In addition, they cautioned being unnecessarily quarantined for 21 days could have negative effects, such as depression or severe stress. Travelers and medical staff were concerned about the prospect of three weeks without work, possibly without pay, upon their return to the United States.

The medical community pointed out health-care professionals like Spencer were keenly aware of the symptoms of Ebola. These people would seek immediate medical treatment and isolation when needed. Some argued requiring a mandatory quarantine was not only unnecessary for medical

"THIS PROTECTIVE MEASURE IS TOO IMPORTANT TO BE VOLUNTARY. WE MUST TAKE EVERY STEP NECESSARY TO ENSURE THE PEOPLE OF ILLINOIS ARE PROTECTED FROM POTENTIAL EXPOSURE TO THE EBOLA VIRUS."[3]

—ILLINOIS GOVERNOR PAT QUINN

professionals who had worked in West Africa, it was insulting.

Spencer said requiring a quarantine was like saying, "We trust you as a public health professional, as a doctor, as a nurse—as someone who is well enough trained to go and fight this disease at its source—but we don't trust you enough to take care of yourself and those around you when you get back."[4]

The Ebola quarantine controversy continued making headlines. It affected the lives of returning health-care professionals, and it fueled public fear of the disease in the United States. It also raised concerns a quarantine would discourage US doctors and nurses from going to fight Ebola at its source.

FEAR VERSUS SCIENCE

When does reasonable concern for public health become unreasonable fear of a potential threat? Many US citizens supported the actions of state governors who enforced mandatory quarantines of people who may have been exposed to Ebola. Others argued such actions reinforced public misunderstanding and led to unnecessary overreactions. For example, a college in Texas rejected applicants from Nigeria because the country had some Ebola cases. In another incident, a teacher in Maine had to take a three-week leave from work because she attended a conference in Dallas, where an Ebola case was diagnosed.

Scientific evidence indicates Ebola virus disease is not easily spread. The virus is transmitted only when an infected person has symptoms of the disease. A person can catch the disease only if the bodily fluids of an infected person enter his or her body. Members of the medical community argued these reasons made the extreme quarantines unnecessary.

CHAPTER EIGHT

HEROES OR
HAZARDS?

The chance of Ebola virus disease spreading in the United States was very slim. Unlike the affected countries in West Africa, the United States has a strong medical system with the necessary resources to combat a potential epidemic. In the United States, fear of the disease became a larger threat than the disease itself.

In November 2014, headlines and news reports featured the story of a nurse who returned from fighting Ebola in West Africa and a governor who imposed a mandatory quarantine. The governor insisted he was acting out of concern for public welfare. Others felt he was acting out of concern for his political

Government attempts to enforce a quarantine on an Ebola-fighting nurse attracted national attention in November 2014.

image, attempting to gain the support of voters whose fear of Ebola was based on misinformation.

THE GOVERNOR AND THE NURSE

Kaci Hickox, a US nurse who worked with MSF to treat Ebola patients in Sierra Leone, returned to the United States on October 24. Her plane landed at Newark Liberty International Airport, where she went through the enhanced screening required for travelers from Ebola-affected countries.

Hickox was detained at the airport for several hours and then informed she was being sent to mandatory quarantine, according to New Jersey guidelines recently announced by Governor Chris Christie.

Hickox argued she had no symptoms, but her temperature was taken several times, and one of the readings indicated she had a fever. She was taken to a hospital, where she was quarantined against her will in a tent outside the building for three days. During that time, she was monitored for symptoms and tested for Ebola. The tests were negative, so Hickox was released on October 27. Hickox believed the mandatory quarantine violated her civil rights since she had no symptoms of Ebola and therefore could not have spread the disease. In an interview, Governor Christie responded, "I understand that she didn't want to be there . . . but my obligation is to all the people of New Jersey and we're just going to continue to do that."[2]

A NATIONAL DEBATE

At her request, Hickox was allowed to leave New Jersey and travel by private car to her home in Maine, but her battle was not over. A few days later, Hickox and her boyfriend made national news when they went on a bike ride—followed by police and journalists. Maine Governor Paul LePage said he would exercise his authority to keep Hickox away from public places. He claimed her behavior was upsetting people, and he said he was trying to protect her as well as the public.

A Maine state trooper trailed Hickox and her boyfriend as they went on their quarantine-defying bike ride.

Governor LePage and state health officials obtained a court order requiring Hickox to remain in her home for the rest of the 21-day quarantine. The nurse challenged the order and won her case. Although the governor could not enforce the order, Hickox agreed to voluntarily avoid public places in order to calm public fears. The nurse stated she had achieved her goal of making the national debate "about science, not politics."[3]

Hickox was not the only Ebola health-care worker viewed as a potential hazard upon returning to the United

States. Spencer monitored himself when he returned home, sought medical help immediately when he became ill, and recovered completely with proper treatment. However, he was accused of being irresponsible because he had gone out in public, even though he showed no symptoms at the time. Hickox never had Ebola, but she was criticized for taking a bike ride within 21 days of returning home.

HONORED AS HEROES

In its December issue, *Time* magazine honored what it called "the Ebola Fighters" as its 2014 Persons of the Year. Articles in the magazine featured individuals from diverse backgrounds who shared the distinction of fighting a war against the most serious Ebola epidemic the world had known.

Stories of heroism inspired gratitude for those who had risked their lives on behalf of strangers. The Ebola fighters taught the value of working as a global community to solve

"THIS WON'T BE THE LAST EPIDEMIC. AND WHEN THE NEXT ONE COMES, THE WORLD MUST LEARN THE LESSONS OF THIS ONE. . . . RUN TOWARD THE FIRE AND PUT IT OUT TOGETHER. . . . REMEMBER THE EBOLA FIGHTERS AND HOPE THAT WE SEE THEIR LIKE AGAIN."[4]

—*TIME* MAGAZINE

The media praised the medical workers who risked contracting Ebola in order to aid people suffering from the disease in West Africa.

problems that have the potential to affect everyone.

Their stories challenged the world to consider the lessons

learned from the Ebola epidemic of 2014.

MORE TO THE
STORY

STORIES OF THE HEROES

In personal interviews, the Ebola fighters shared their motivations and their experiences. They had diverse backgrounds and jobs, and each had a role to play in the struggle against the disease.

Katie Meyler is an American who founded More Than Me, a school for girls in Monrovia, Liberia. When the Ebola epidemic hit, the mission of the school changed from educating young girls to keeping them alive. Meyler shared a story about rescuing a child named Esther who survived Ebola only to discover her entire family had died of the disease. Meyler said, "When you say 'Ebola' to me, I think about Esther."[5]

Salome Karwah, a trainee nurse at her parents' medical clinic near Monrovia, survived Ebola, but she watched both of her parents die of the disease. When MSF sought Ebola survivors to work in its treatment centers, Karwah volunteered. "Sitting and crying won't help me," Karwah said. "So I decided to make myself very much busy to help others survive."[6]

Brantly testified in front of a congressional committee about his experiences with Ebola.

FIRSTHAND EXPERIENCE

Brantly survived Ebola, and he learned a great deal from his experiences. He knew firsthand what it felt like to have the disease: "My body began shaking, my heart was racing. Nothing would bring down my temperature, and I had fluid in my lungs. I felt hot, nauseated, weak—everything was a blur."[7]

Brantly also understood the aftereffects of the disease: "After a day of activity, I would be totally wiped out. I'd be dizzy, nauseated, even felt a little feverish at times. I was incredibly fatigued."[8]

Although other survivors returned to West Africa to continue their work, Brantly remained in the United States.

Based on his experiences, Brantly was in a unique position to influence public opinion and government action. In West Africa, he would be treating dozens of patients a day. Instead, Brantly decided to meet with influential groups in the United States. By speaking about what needed to be done to combat Ebola, he hoped to benefit thousands of people.

Brantly appeared on television and radio programs, and he testified before Congress on behalf of the Ebola victims in West Africa. In his book, *Called for Life: How Loving Our Neighbor Led Us into the Heart of the Ebola Epidemic*, Brantly provides insight into his own experiences and encourages concern for the welfare of others.

RETURNING TO BATTLE

Nancy Writebol left Emory Hospital after treatment for Ebola in August 2014. She spoke about her work in Liberia, her battle with Ebola, and her commitment to the people of West Africa. As an Ebola survivor, Nancy was thought to be immune to the disease. She donated blood to help treat others with Ebola. Nancy's husband David volunteered to test an experimental vaccine. In March 2015, the Writebols returned to Liberia to continue the fight against Ebola.

For many years, Dr. Rick Sacra divided his time between working in West Africa and being with his family in Massachusetts. In August 2014, he returned to Liberia to fill a need for doctors to care for patients without Ebola. Sacra contracted Ebola while working in a maternity hospital. He was brought back to the United States for treatment, and he recovered. In January 2015, Sacra returned to Liberia to continue his work.

CHAPTER NINE

OUTLOOK: 2015
AND BEYOND

T he Ebola crisis in West Africa dominated headlines throughout the world for many months in 2014. By the end of that year, the number of new cases diminished, and Ebola was no longer front-page news. But the battle was not over. A much smaller flare-up of the disease was reported in early 2015, reminding the world it takes only one case to restart an outbreak.

In January 2015, the WHO announced its response to Ebola had shifted from slowing the epidemic to ending it completely. Getting to zero cases required detecting every new case and managing it as effectively as possible. The presence of any case in any country created the risk of another outbreak.

Liberia was declared free of Ebola in May 2015, but the threat of another major outbreak still loomed over the region.

"WE RUN THE RISK OF GOING FROM HYSTERIA TO A SENSE OF INDIFFERENCE. AND I THINK THAT IS EVEN MORE DANGEROUS THAN OUR FEAR—WHEN WE STOP CARING ABOUT WHAT'S HAPPENING ON THE OTHER SIDE OF THE WORLD."[1]

—DR. KENT BRANTLY

Despite the progress made in the fight against Ebola, many challenges remained. The spring rainy season interfered with control efforts. Mud and floods made remote areas difficult to reach and prevented people from seeking medical care. To achieve the goal of stopping Ebola, a continued international effort was required. Lessons learned from the 2014 epidemic guided the fight against Ebola in 2015 and beyond.

In April 2015, President Obama met with African leaders to discuss the progress made in stopping Ebola.

THE TOLL OF THE 2014 EPIDEMIC

The total number of deaths resulting from the Ebola epidemic was difficult to determine, partly because the number was constantly increasing and partly because many deaths went unreported. By the end of December 2014, the WHO estimated a global death toll of approximately 7,500 out of 19,500 cases.[2] Later, more accurate reports increased these figures. By May 2015, the CDC estimated more than 11,000 deaths out of nearly 27,000 cases.[3] The death toll continued to rise in 2015, but at a much lower rate than before.

In addition to the devastating loss of human life, the Ebola epidemic had other serious consequences. The disease became a global

POST-EBOLA SYNDROME

As new cases of Ebola declined in West Africa, attention turned to a different group of patients—Ebola survivors. People who recovered from Ebola continued to suffer from a variety of medical problems that became known as post-Ebola syndrome. Their symptoms included weakness, tiredness, muscle pain, headaches, and vision problems. These people required ongoing medical care, but this was a new situation. Medical science had no previous studies on which to base treatment.

In addition to the physical problems, many survivors suffered from grief for lost family members and friends. They often faced economic problems from loss of jobs or inability to work. Some suffered discrimination from communities that would not accept them. Many of the same local and international organizations that helped battle the disease set up programs to help the survivors.

concern, but the places that were hardest hit—Guinea, Liberia, and Sierra Leone—were among the world's poorest countries. Fighting Ebola caused the collapse of their health systems and further stressed their economies. As a result, many people died of treatable diseases, such as malaria and pneumonia, because they could not receive treatment.

ECONOMIC IMPACT

West African industries, such as mining, suffered because companies stopped operations and sent workers home for fear of the disease. As a result, foreign investments decreased. A decline in economic activity reduced the amount of money governments received. At the same time, governments needed more money to help fight the Ebola crisis.

The World Bank is an international banking organization that monitors economic activity and provides financial assistance to countries in times of crisis. In 2014, it noted the largest economic effects of the Ebola crisis were based on fear. Closing the hot zone to tourists caused a decline in tourism in other parts of Africa because travelers

Once-popular tourist destinations, such as the beaches of Robertsport, Liberia, were nearly empty during the worst of the Ebola crisis.

feared the spread of the disease. Fear of Ebola also reduced the labor force, closed places of employment, and disrupted trade between countries.

LESSONS LEARNED

January 2015 marked one year after the recognized beginning of the Ebola outbreak in West Africa. In order to develop a plan for moving forward, experts and international organizations reviewed the events of 2014. They learned several important lessons from the outbreak.

First, they recognized the importance of strong health systems. Guinea, Sierra Leone, and Liberia have weak health systems. Many people in those countries do not have access to basic health care for diseases, even for those that can be cured, such as malaria. The sudden outbreak of a deadly virus overwhelmed the limited health systems. Without the necessary resources, these systems failed when they were needed most. What began as a local health crisis grew into a regional social and economic crisis and eventually into a global crisis.

Experts also noted the necessity of being prepared. Closely related to the weak health systems in the hot-zone countries was a lack of preparedness. Ebola virus disease was unknown in West Africa when the first cases arrived. Health systems were unprepared to isolate sick patients and get a prompt diagnosis. This allowed the disease to spread out of control. In contrast, Nigeria, Senegal, and Mali had good systems in place with strong laboratory support. Health officials were prepared to take swift action to control the spread of the disease in their countries.

The effectiveness of strict controls was seen as another key factor in reducing the spread of the disease. The Ebola epidemic was a complex emergency that required several control measures. Ebola victims had to be isolated, all contacts had to be traced and monitored for symptoms, and safe burial practices had to be enforced. In addition, health-care workers had to adequately protect themselves from the disease. They also had to use proper hygiene within treatment facilities to avoid spreading the disease. When one of these measures broke down, the rest were unsuccessful.

Finally, medical experts saw the value of gaining community support through public awareness and education. Fear and ignorance were two of the biggest obstacles in the fight against Ebola. Many people in the hot zone did not trust doctors and did not seek medical care. They hid Ebola patients in their homes and continued practices

PROGRESS ON EBOLA TREATMENT AND PREVENTION

In February 2015, clinical trials for ZMapp started in Liberia. Any adult or child infected with Ebola could enroll in the trial. Health-care workers sent to the United States for treatment were also eligible. The participants were divided into two groups. Both groups received the best care possible for the disease, but one group also received three doses of ZMapp given three days apart. The results of the trial would determine whether or not ZMapp was an effective treatment for Ebola.

In April 2015, Ebola vaccine trials began in Sierra Leone. The trial involved 6,000 health-care workers who were working with Ebola patients.[4] Participants were divided into two groups. The first group received the vaccine immediately; the second group was scheduled to receive it six months later. Then all participants would be monitored for six months to determine if the vaccine was effective in preventing Ebola.

As the epidemic slowed in early 2015, the WHO and other organizations celebrated the progress but prepared for the possibility of future outbreaks.

that spread the disease. People did not understand why they could not stay with sick family members or take care of them. They had to be convinced not to use traditional methods of preparing bodies for burial.

A PLAN FOR THE FUTURE

The lessons learned from the 2014 outbreak indicated the importance of developing a plan to fight future outbreaks. Opinions differed about how to put a plan in place and which problems to concentrate on first. Medical experts and health organizations strongly agreed on two points: the battle against Ebola was not over, and there was no time to lose in preparing a defense.

Investing in stronger health-care systems in low-income countries is essential to the fight against Ebola and diseases like it. Countries continue to need international support and assistance to rebuild their health services and provide facilities where they are most needed. Public confidence in the health systems that protect and heal people must be restored.

Being prepared for future outbreaks involves increasing research aimed at developing drugs and vaccines. Ebola virus had been identified decades before the 2014 outbreak, but no effective medicines had been developed, tested, and approved. The urgent need for prevention and treatment encouraged funding for research. The development of vaccines for Ebola must be balanced by the need for drugs to treat other diseases that might threaten global health in the future.

Controlling the spread of Ebola involves both medical and social issues. The 2014 epidemic gave doctors a better understanding of the virus and ways to keep it from spreading. In the second phase of the fight against Ebola, MSF used mobile teams to locate new cases. They treated each case as a potential epidemic. They used all the strategies that had proved effective—isolation, tracing and monitoring contacts, and creating public awareness. They remained cautiously hopeful these efforts would help them make progress toward the goal of zero cases. By February 2015, the number of new cases of Ebola declined from more than 1,000 per week to approximately 150 per week.[5] The number varied due to periodic flare-ups, but the total was significantly reduced.

The social issues required changing people's behaviors. An awareness campaign was needed to inform people about the disease and encourage them to cooperate with local health requirements. The cooperation of local leaders and public health workers was essential to gaining people's trust. The people in West African communities changed their traditional practices at the request of trusted local leaders. Moving forward, local health officials can influence people to participate in prevention and treatment for infectious diseases.

"WE'VE BEEN RUNNING BEHIND EBOLA SINCE THE BEGINNING; TODAY IT FINALLY SEEMS POSSIBLE TO CATCH UP. THIS IS DEFINITELY NOT THE TIME TO REST."[6]

—MARIA TERESA CACCIAPOUTI, HEAD OF THE MSF MISSION IN LIBERIA

In early 2015, MSF began to dismantle its large Ebola treatment facilities.

CHALLENGES AHEAD

In December 2014, the *Time* article honoring Ebola fighters stated, "There is hope. And hope has proved to be the most potent weapon yet discovered against Ebola."[7] The reasons for hope included a decline in the number of cases of Ebola in West Africa and an increase in survival rates. Nations had responded to a global crisis. The Ebola fighters had made a difference.

Despite the progress made by early 2015, experts warned the fight against Ebola was not over. Many challenges remained ahead. The WHO took responsibility for mistakes in handling the response to the Ebola outbreak. It outlined a plan for future emergencies that included increasing preparedness and coordinating local and international efforts. Implementing the plan would mean that the next time an Ebola outbreak occurs, governments and aid organizations would be ready to fight back.

Aid organizations created informational posters to educate people on ways to protect themselves from Ebola.

ESSENTIAL
FACTS

MAJOR EVENTS

- In December 2013, a two-year-old boy becomes patient zero for the deadliest Ebola epidemic in history.

- In March 2014, health authorities in West Africa recognize the Ebola epidemic.

- In August 2014, two US health workers diagnosed with Ebola virus disease are flown to the United States for treatment.

- In January 2015, the goal of medical authorities shifts from slowing the outbreak to ending it completely.

KEY PLAYERS

- International groups such as Doctors Without Borders, the World Health Organization, and Samaritan's Purse become among the first sources of aid for Ebola-stricken communities in West Africa.

- US medical workers Kent Brantly and Nancy Writebol contract Ebola virus disease and are flown home for treatment.

- Thomas Eric Duncan is the first patient to die of Ebola virus disease in the United States.

- US nurse Kaci Hickox challenges government attempts to force her into a quarantine.

IMPACT ON SOCIETY

The Ebola epidemic of 2014 claimed the lives of thousands of people in West Africa. It overtaxed health-care systems in the affected regions, showing the need for better facilities and procedures to fight future outbreaks. The outbreak spurred widespread fear in the United States, despite the extremely unlikely chance of it spreading within the country. It also sparked debates about the role of governments in enforcing quarantines based on scientific evidence rather than public fears.

QUOTE

"My body began shaking, my heart was racing. Nothing would bring down my temperature, and I had fluid in my lungs. I felt hot, nauseated, weak—everything was a blur."

—Dr. Kent Brantly

GLOSSARY

ANTIBODY
A protein the body produces to destroy bacteria or viruses that cause diseases.

CONTAGIOUS
Spreading easily from one organism to another.

EPIDEMIOLOGIST
A scientists who studies the spread of disease.

HOT ZONE
A particularly dangerous area in which people require protection from infectious diseases.

HYGIENE
Practices that preserve or promote health.

PLACEBO
A substance that has no effect on the body and is given to patients in clinical studies to compare against the effectiveness of real medicines.

RESERVOIR HOST

The source of an infection.

SPILLOVER

The process of a virus being transmitted from an animal to a human.

SYMPTOM

A sign or indication of a disease.

VACCINE

A substance given to a person to train his or her immune system to fight a disease.

VIRUS

A microscopic organism that can cause disease.

ADDITIONAL
RESOURCES

SELECTED BIBLIOGRAPHY

Baker, Aryn. "Racing Ebola: What the World Needs to Do to Stop the Deadly Virus." *Time* 13 Oct. 2014: 38–45. Print

Piot, Peter. *No Time to Lose*. New York: Norton, 2012. Print.

Preston, Von Drehle, David, and Aryn Baker. "The Ones Who Answered the Call." *Time* 22/29 Dec. 2014: 70–107. Print.

FURTHER READINGS

Hand, Carol. *Epidemiology: The Fight Against Ebola and Other Diseases*. Minneapolis, MN: Abdo, 2015. Print.

Hirschmann, Kris. *The Ebola Virus*. Detroit, MI: Lucent, 2007. Print

Peters, Marilee. *Patient Zero: Solving the Mysteries of Deadly Epidemics*. Toronto, Canada: Annick, 2014. Print.

WEBSITES

To learn more about Special Reports, visit **booklinks.abdopublishing.com**. These links are routinely monitored and updated to provide the most current information available.

FOR MORE INFORMATION

For more information on this subject, contact or visit the following organizations:

Centers for Disease Control and Prevention (CDC)
1600 Clifton Road
Atlanta, GA 30329
800-CDC-INFO
http://www.cdc.gov
The CDC provides facts and statistics about diseases, information about global health topics, and travel health notices. The website provides easy access to Ebola topics and updates.

Doctors Without Borders/Médecins Sans Frontières (MSF)
333 Seventh Avenue
New York, NY 10001
212-679-6800
http://www.doctorswithoutborders.org
Doctors Without Borders is a source of information about international projects, medical and social issues, and research. The website provides videos and slideshows of the organization in action as well as Ebola updates.

SOURCE NOTES

CHAPTER 1. OUTBREAK 2014

1. Drew Hinshaw. "Healthcare Workers Die for Want of Basic Supplies." *Wall Street Journal*. Wall Street Journal, 3 Oct. 2014. Web. 17 Mar. 2015.

2. "Physician Density in West African Countries Suffering from the 2014 Ebola Outbreak." *Statista*. Statista, 2015. Web. 17 Mar. 2015.

3. Aryn Baker. "Racing Ebola: What the World Needs to Do to Stop the Deadly Virus." *Time*. Time, 2 Oct. 2014. Web. 11 June 2015.

4. "Ebola Outbreak: A Timeline of the Worst Epidemic of the Virulent Disease in History." *Reuters*. Reuters, 29 Nov. 2014. Web. 14 Mar. 2015.

5. Ibid.

6. Grady, Denise and Sheri Fink. "Tracing Ebola's Breakout to an African 2-Year-Old." *New York Times*. New York Times, 9 Aug. 2014. Web. 15 Mar. 2015.

7. "WHO Declares End of Ebola Outbreak in Nigeria." *World Health Organization*. World Health Organization, 20 Oct. 2014. Web. 25 Apr. 2015.

8. Nassos Stylianou. "How World's Worst Ebola Outbreak Began with One Boy's Death." *BBC News*. BBC, 26 Nov. 2014. Web. 16 Mar. 2015.

CHAPTER 2. TRACING THE HISTORY OF A VIRUS

1. Alexandra Sifferlin. "Ebola: The First Glimpse of a Virus." *Time*. Time, 13 Oct. 2014. Web. 25 Apr. 2015.

2. Peter Piot. *No Time to Lose*. New York: Norton, 2012. Print. 37.

3. Richard Preston. *The Hot Zone*. New York: Random, 1994. Print. 71.

4. "Ebola Haemorrhagic Fever in Sudan, 1976." *Bulletin of the World Health Organization*. World Health Organization, 1978. Web. 5 Mar. 2015.

5. "Ebola Virus Disease." *World Health Organization*. World Health Organization, Apr. 2015. Web. 11 June 2015.

6. "Chronology of Previous Ebola Virus Disease Outbreaks." *World Health Organization*. World Health Organization, Sept. 2014. Web. 17 Mar. 2015.

7. Julia Belluz. "The Man Who Discovered Ebola on Why This Epidemic Spiraled out of Control." *Vox.* Vox. 29 Sept. 2014. Web. 18 Mar. 2015.

CHAPTER 3. RESPONDING TO THE CRISIS

1. Laurie Garrett. "You Are Not Nearly Scared Enough about Ebola." *Foreign Policy Magazine.* Foreign Policy Magazine, 15 Aug. 2014. Web. 28 Feb. 2015.

2. "Grim Ebola Prediction: Outbreak Is 'Unstoppable' For Now, Says US Virologist." *Live Science.* Live Science, 5 Sept. 2014. Web. 25 Apr. 2015.

3. Jonathan Oatis. "Chronology—Worst Ebola Outbreak on Record Tests Global Response." *Reuters.* Reuters, 28 Oct. 2014. Web. 25 Apr. 2015.

4. Mark Landler and Somini Sengupta. "Global Response to Ebola Is Too Slow, Obama Warns." *New York Times.* New York Times, 25 Sept. 2014. Web. 19 Mar. 2015.

5. Ibid.

6. Zeke J. Miller. "US to Commit $500 Million, Deploy 3,000 Troops in Ebola Fight." *Time.* Time, 16 Sept. 2014. Web. 11 June 2015.

7. Aryn Baker. "Racing Ebola: What the World Needs to Do to Stop the Deadly Virus." *Time.* Time, 2 Oct. 2014. Web. 11 June 2015.

8. Laurie Garrett. "You Are Not Nearly Scared Enough about Ebola." *Foreign Policy Magazine.* Foreign Policy Magazine, 15 Aug. 2014. Web. 28 Feb. 2015.

9. Mary Jane Skala. "US Army Pfc. Gilbertson Put Fears Aside to Help Build Ebola Treatment Centers in Liberia." *Kearney Hub.* Kearney Hub, 7 Mar. 2015. Web. 29 Mar. 2015.

10. Ibid.

11. "UN Mission for Ebola Emergency Response." *United Nations Information Center.* United Nations, 30 Jan. 2015. Web. 25 Apr. 2015.

12. "How Many Ebola Patients Have Been Treated Outside of Africa?" *New York Times.* New York Times, 26 Jan. 2015. Web. 19 Mar. 2015.

CHAPTER 4. A GLOBAL THREAT

1. Betsy Klein. "Ebola Is a 'National Security Priority,' Obama Says." *CNN.* CNN, 8 Sept. 2014. Web. 12 June 2015.

2. Jonathan Cohn. "Most Ebola Patients in the US Survive. Half in Africa Die. Why Are We Letting This Happen?" *New Republic.* New Republic, 29 Oct. 2014. Web. 20 Mar. 2015.

3. "2014 Ebola Outbreak in West Africa – Case Counts." *CDC.* CDC, 22 July 2015. Web. 22 July 2015.

SOURCE NOTES
CONTINUED

CHAPTER 5. JUST THE FACTS, PLEASE

1. David Quammen. *Spillover.* New York: Norton, 2012. Print. 115–116.

CHAPTER 6. THERE IS NO CURE

1. James Gallagher. "Ebola: Experimental Drug ZMapp Is '100% Effective' in Animal Trials." *BBC News.* BBC, 29 Aug. 2014. Web. 23 Mar. 2015.

CHAPTER 7. QUARANTINE CONTROVERSY

1. Rachel Brody. "Quarantine US Soldiers, Says DOD." *US News and World Report.* US News and World Report, 29 Oct. 2014. Web. 12 June 2015.

2. "History of Quarantine." *CDC.* CDC, n.d. Web. 30 Mar. 2015.

3. Sydney Lupkin. "Why There's So Much Controversy Surrounding Ebola Quarantine Orders." *ABC News.* ABC, n.d. Web. 28 Feb. 2015.

4. "After Surviving Ebola, Craig Spencer Still Feels 'Violated' by America's Needless Panic." *PRI.* PRI, 2 Feb. 2015. Web. 23 Mar. 2015.

CHAPTER 8. HEROES OR HAZARDS?

1. "Dr. Kent Brantly: Lessons Learned from Fighting Ebola." *NPR.* NPR, 15 Dec. 2014. Web. 5 Mar. 2015.

2. Josh Margolin and Meghan Keneally. "Ebola Nurse Kaci Hickox Will 'Understand' Her Quarantine, New Jersey Governor Says." *ABC News.* ABC, 27 Oct. 2014. Web. 23 Mar. 2015.

3. John Bacon. "Maine Nurse Gives Ground on Ebola Quarantine." *USA Today.* USA Today, 2 Nov. 2014. Web. 1 Mar. 2015.

4. David Von Drehle and Aryn Baker. "The Ones Who Answered the Call." *Time.* Time, 10 Dec. 2014. Web. 12 June 2015.

5. Ibid.

6. Ibid.

7. Kent Brantly. "This Is What It Feels Like to Survive Ebola." *Time*. Time, 5 Sept. 2014. Web. 5 Mar. 2015.

8. "Dr. Kent Brantly: Lessons Learned from Fighting Ebola." *NPR*. NPR, 15 Dec. 2014. Web. 5 Mar. 2015.

CHAPTER 9. OUTLOOK: 2015 AND BEYOND

1. "Dr. Kent Brantly: Lessons Learned from Fighting Ebola." *NPR*. NPR, 15 Dec. 2014. Web. 5 Mar. 2015.

2. "Death Toll in Ebola Outbreak Rises to 7,588: WHO." *Reuters*. Reuters, 24 Dec. 2014. Web. 24 Mar. 2015.

3. "2014 Ebola Outbreak in West Africa – Case Counts." *CDC*. CDC, 11 June 2015. Web. 12 June 2015.

4. "Ebola Vaccine Trial Begins in Sierra Leone." *CDC*. CDC, 14 Apr. 2015. Web. 29 Apr. 2015.

5. "Fact Sheet: Progress in Our Ebola Response at Home and Abroad." *White House*. White House, 11 Feb. 2015. Web. 31 Mar. 2015.

6. "'This Is Definitely Not the Time to Rest' on Ebola." *MSF*. MSF, 13 Feb. 2015. Web. 28 Feb. 2015.

7. David Von Drehle and Aryn Baker. "The Ones Who Answered the Call." *Time*. Time, 10 Dec. 2014. Web. 12 June 2015.

INDEX

ABOUT THE
AUTHOR

Carolee Laine is an educator and children's writer. She has written social studies textbooks and other educational materials as well as passages for statewide assessments. She enjoys learning through researching and writing nonfiction books for young readers. Carolee lives in the Chicago suburbs.

ABOUT THE CONSULTANT

Ana Ayala is the global health law LL.M. program director at Georgetown University's O'Neill Institute for National and Global Health Law. Since joining the institute in 2010, Ana has worked to use the law to advance public health goals in a number of areas, including infectious diseases and global health governance. Originally from Bolivia, Ana received her master of laws (LL.M.) in global health law from Georgetown University; her law degree from American University; and her bachelor of arts degree in anthropology and international studies from the University of Chicago.